Proud of Me?

*Lessons Learned by the Father
of a Special-Needs Child*

Brad Russell

CrossHouse

Published by
CROSSHOUSE PUBLISHING
PO Box 461592
Garland, Texas 75046-1592
www.crosshousepublishing.org
1-877-212-0933

Printed in the United States of America
by Lightning Source, LaVergne, TN
Cover design by Dennis Davidson

ISBN 978-1-934749-77-7
Library of Congress Control Number: 2010926531

TO ORDER ADDITIONAL COPIES, SEE PAGE 79

I dedicate this book
to my beautiful wife, Robin, the love of
my life for more than 32 years and a
wonderful mother to our three children,
Tyler, Timothy, and Emily.

Table of Contents

Acknowledgements

I want to thank some people for their encouragement in my writing this book.

My wife, Robin, is the love of my life. While we dated when we were teenagers, she pointed me to Jesus. She helped me to find the truth. She has the caring touch and compassion that children need in a family, especially when a special-needs child lives with them. Her abilities are gifts from God. The Lord never let up on us to finish what He started on our wedding day.

Our other children, Timothy and Emily, have been examples of how to love a brother with special needs and to trust Jesus for the results of that love. Timothy and Emily, now adults, have encouraged us and been a source of strength for us to rely on no matter what. This story would not have been possible without the love and support of both of them. Their arms always have been around us; we know they smile when they think of "Big Brother" Tyler.

I also thank my parents, John and Charlene, and Robin's parents, A.L. and Virginia, who always set an example for me by the way they cared for others. I am so proud of them. I also will never forget the smiles and conversations that took place over the years between Tyler and his grandparents.

And last but not least, to all of the people who accept

as blessings from God special-needs children into their homes and lives, you, too, are my heroes. I am so *"proud of you!"*

INTRODUCTION

As you look back on your life, I hope you had many times when you wanted to do something that would make your dad proud of you. Maybe it was so he would look at you and smile, or just say, "Good job." Or maybe you truly wanted him to use the words, "I am proud of you." This certainly was an important desire in my own life. I wanted my dad to be proud of me.

Now that I am an adult and a father of three, I know even more the importance of these five words—"I am proud of you"—in a child's life. What makes my story different is that I also know first hand how much more important these affirmative words are to a child with special needs.

Robin and I never planned to have a special-needs child. We just wanted to be parents. We wanted to be like all other parents with so-called "normal" children. But God had other plans for us.

Robin and I have three beautiful children—Tyler, Timothy, and Emily. Each is special to us. We love all three dearly, even though their abilities and life circumstances differ widely.

When Tyler, our oldest, was diagnosed with cerebral palsy, we began to weather a storm far more intense than we ever could have imagined. What we didn't realize, though, was that this storm would open our eyes to see

God in brand new ways—ways we might have missed had our son not had these challenges.

One of the ways God has spoken to us is through the very words of our challenged child. Even though the doctors said Tyler might not ever speak, the Lord had other plans. Tyler can speak in short phrases and broken sentences. I have organized this book so that each chapter title is a word or phrase that throughout the years has become very familiar to us—as they are the exact words spoken by our special son. Although the phrases are short, they are as much to the point about life as any normal sentence in a meaningful conversation could ever be. I hope you will enjoy reading his words as much as I enjoy hearing them and using them in this book. I hope you will discover as I have that God's glory is sometimes revealed in the simplest of ways.

To help you understand some of the things I want to say to you, let me go back now and tell you my story from the beginning.

First, I want to share one of those times when I am convinced my dad was proud of me. When I was 12-years old, I attended a youth meeting at our church. The leader at our table asked us questions about life. The man asked us boys, "How far would you go with a girl?" I clearly remember saying I would go to the "Dairy Queen with her." I was thinking of the ice-cream shop close to our church. I will never forget my dad's smile after he heard my response.

While I desired my father's affirmation, I confess that for a while during my teenage years I lost that desire. Before and after those years, his words of affirmation were very important to me.

Can you relate to how important my dad's affirmation was to me then? I certainly hope you can. And maybe even as to how as a typical teenager I wanted somewhat to distance myself from my dad and mom? I bet many of you can relate to this, too.

When on July 22, 1978, Robin and I first said, "I do", life ahead looked so incredibly blissful and beautiful. Our view of the world was like the weather that day— clear, sunny, and calm. I will never forget that day! Our families were there cheering us on. We had made so many plans for our life together—including our children's names to pass out at the appropriate times and a love for each other that never would be broken. The last part, the love, is true.

If I could paint for you a picture of our wedding day, it would look a lot like the way in which Jesus says to His disciples, *"let us go to the other side"* (Mark 4:35). Like the disciples on that day all the members of my family— Robin, our sons Tyler and Timothy, and our daughter Emily—have all chosen to get into the boat with Jesus and travel with Him to *"the other side"*. For many years our family has sailed the seas with Jesus.

Also, like the disciples on that day, our family has encountered surprising and difficult weather patterns. The Bible says in Mark 4:37, *and there arose a fierce gale of wind, and the waves were breaking over the boat so much that the boat was already filling up.*

This was like the same thing that occurred to all of us. Robin and I set sail for a life on a placid, calm sea, but we soon encountered strong winds and rough waves that brought about the diagnosis given our oldest child.

When the storm happened to the disciples on the boat that day, they ran to the place in which Jesus was situated on the boat. They found Him asleep. *"Teacher, do you not care that we are perishing?"* they cried out to Jesus. By getting up and rebuking the wind and calming the storm, Jesus showed them He cared.

That's exactly what Jesus has done in our lives. The One True Source of hope and peace in our boat has been Jesus. He has always been there for us. He always calms the storms of life. I confess, however, that I am still learning to trust Him and let Him have his way with my family and me.

Brain damage during the birth process caused our first son, Tyler, to be born with cerebral palsy. When he was a few months old, we learned about his condition. Today he has an IQ of 36 and needs leg braces to walk. He is 28-years old and still lives with us. When he was 13-months old, we were told that he might never talk or walk, yet today he does both but in less than perfect ways. Nevertheless, God continues to use Tyler to encourage others with his smiles and these terse sentences.

Our other son is Timothy. He is the best "big brother" to Tyler that you can imagine. He is a married to Amber. She is a wonderful sister-in-law to Tyler, too. Timothy and Amber live close by us so Tyler gets to see them as often as possible.

Emily is our daughter. She is Tyler's "sweet girl" and his biggest fan!

So you see we have a lot in common with most

people. We just happen to have one special-needs child and two very special "normal" adult children. We are an average, middle-class family from the Midwest. We believe in the family as God designed it to be.

Where we seem to differ from many in our culture and in our situation is in the area of divorce. We all know that families are in trouble today, but when a family has a child with special needs, the rate of divorce for them sky-rockets. That's sad but true. Having a special-needs child puts lots of pressure on families. Sadly, often dads of special-needs children leave their wives and their special children. They apparently can't cope with the extra responsibilities and unusual stress that having a special-needs child creates. This pattern is not improving. Fortunately that did not happen in our case.

My story is about how God can use a child who arrives in the form of a storm but who ultimately helps bring to his family peace, calm, and a sense of closeness to God. This probably is not how most of the world would view our situation. Others may see only the work, the stress, and the heightened responsibilities innate in our situation. We, however, are experiencing growth from it and have made it work. God is holding us together. Without God's help, Robin and I would be broken apart and have no hope or a successful marriage. Only by His grace and presence in our lives are we able to see the other side of this story. This book was written partially to remind all three of our children how proud I am of them. I also wrote this book to ask whether they've been proud of me for sticking with it and putting my hand to the oar all these years.

When I was 10, my grandmother asked me why I did-n't write more letters to her. She said she thought I wrote "good ones." Back in those days all I wanted to do was tell my grandmother how great I felt about being a kid and how special she was to me. I also wanted her to know what was going on in my life at the time. Not long ago I found some of those letters. My grandmother had given them to my mom. As I read them, I recalled the positive feelings I had in writing them. While re-reading them again as an adult I enjoyed not only my own pleas-ure but the laughter of other family members who also had gathered at the time to view some old pictures of us that Grandma had.

I really hope that as you read these very simple words about our family, you will experience positive feelings, smiles, and laughter. My prayer is that you will be encouraged by reading this book.

Remember: Our hope is in Jesus, not the things of this world. By faith in Him—and the grace that we have because of the cross—we were able to climb into the boat with Jesus and begin our journey to the other side. His invitation is issued to all of us. Because of His great love for humanity, Jesus offers salvation to us all.

I hope this testimony of what we have seen and heard in "our boat" will be an encouragement to you. I also hope you no matter the weather will let Him captain your boat to the other side.

Chapter 1

HAPPENED?

Anytime we want to know what just occurred or to help us better understand a situation or circumstance in life we all ask the question "What happened?". Tyler's shortened way of saying this is *"Happened?"*

Tyler is extremely interested in all aspects of the lives of his family members—whether he hears about something first-, second-, or even third-hand. He will say *"Happened?"* when any of us get off the phone after we have a conversation with someone; he wants to know what we discussed. If he sees, hears, or senses a sign of trouble in the situation, he will quickly say, *"Tell Jesus?"*

About nine years ago I discovered something in God's Word that made a major impact on my life. This revelation was so exciting I kept thinking about it constantly. This insight began while I was reading the statement Jesus made to His disciples in Mark 4:35-41. These verses contain a promise I never before had seen. The Scripture says, *on the same day, when evening had come, He said to them, "Let us cross over to the other side." Now when they had left the multitude they took Him along in the boat as He was. And other little boats were also with Him. And a great windstorm arose, and the waves beat into the boat, so that it was already filling. But He was in the stern, asleep on a pillow. And they awoke Him and said to Him, "Teacher, do you not care that we are perishing?" Then He arose and rebuked the wind, and said to the sea, "Peace be still! " And the wind ceased and there was a great calm. But He said to them, "Why are you so fearful? How is it that you have no faith?" They feared exceedingly, and said to one another, "Who can this be, that even the winds and the sea obey Him?"*

What struck me deep in my heart is that what *"Happened?"* to those closest to Him is that they ended up forgetting the very first thing He had said to them. He had said, *"Let us cross over to the other side."* This was a promise He was giving to them. I believe He was giving this promise to the disciples that day but also to anyone who receives His free gift of eternal life and is in the boat "with Him." They were going to the other side, and so are we! This was our life! This was our trip with Jesus!

I am not one to discuss the weather all the time, but it suddenly occurred to me that this passage is all about the weather. Storms *"happen"* while we sail with Jesus in His boat or without Him in our own boat all alone — tossed back and forth with every circumstance of life. He was about to teach me how much I could doubt Him and His ability to keep me safe in the midst of a raging storm.

I can identify with the disciples very well. The weather seemed so very bright and beautiful that July day in 1978. Robin and I had just become man and wife. Out before us all we could see was blue sky. Our wedding day was simply the best day of our lives! We had committed our marriage to God and had the brightest of futures in the Lord's boat. I was in sales and Robin was finishing college in Pittsburg, KS. We had been dating for about six years, so we knew everything there was to know about each other, or so we thought. Certainly nothing appeared to be "out there" on that glassy calm of a lake to rock our steady ship as we headed out to sea. What *"happens"* on the sea is that weather is always there. It can range in nature from peaceful and mild with an absolutely beautiful sunshine to the most rough and upsetting storm imaginable. We didn't realize how high the waves could rise, nor did we know how awesome our Lord would be in calming them.

According to Tyler—a young man that the world might easily say represents some real rough weather— what *"happens"* after it gets dark is that the sun comes out. It always does! Our experiences these past 28 years have been about learning love, joy, peace, longsuffering, gentleness, goodness, faith, meekness, and temperance. These are the fruits of the Spirit. We can only learn them in our ship on the sea with Jesus, not in our own boats without His presence. Here is what *"happened"*.

Tyler was born Feb. 11, 1982, in Pittsburg, KS. This was an awesome day for Robin and me. Like other fathers before me, I was particularly proud that I was the father of a first-born son. Most men who have fathered their first sons could identify with my feelings that day. My sense of pride in what just *"happened"* was staggering. I could envision tossing baseballs and footballs to my son, taking him on long bike rides, and doing all the millions of other things fathers and sons love to do together. In my dreams I watched and cheered him from the stadium stands as he exhibited his athletic prowess.

At this point things began to change. The delivery became more difficult than normal. At times during labor Tyler's heart rate dropped low. The concern I saw on the faces of the nurses and the doctor was very disturbing to me. I was worried but just tried to pray for Robin and Tyler to be OK.

"Happened?" While I was basking in the future sunlight and had great plans for our new son, the skies were growing darker, but we at first didn't know it. What did we know? He was our first-born. We loved him dearly. *"Proud of me?"* Of course we were!

Robin is a great mom and very observant. Her love for her family is an awesome witness to others of how strong our Lord is in life. Tyler was not real late in saying his first word, which I think was "dada". Robin, however, noticed that Tyler was not at six to eight months sitting up like he should have been. More puzzling was the fact that he liked to pull himself up to the windows to look out and crawled by using his arms. He was getting stronger in his upper body, but his legs were very weak.

Tyler's smile was there from the beginning, but mine was fading. I was thinking how strong I thought I was, but I began instead to understand my helplessness. Clouds began to appear on the horizon. The sun was moving slowly behind them. A cool breeze was turning into bitterly cold chills.

"Happened?" We were about to be tossed to and fro. We felt as though Jesus was asleep in the stern! When Tyler was about 13-months old and still not standing or

sitting up on his own, we made an appointment for Tyler with a specialist. I was beginning to lose sight of the dreams I had of running with him and spending precious time watching him do all those activities that kids participate in. As the doctor completed his examination of Tyler and began to deliver his diagnosis, I did everything but cover my ears when he told us that our son had cerebral palsy and most likely would never walk and probably would never talk. I remember so vividly sitting in that corner examining room on the second floor and wondering how this could be *"happening"* to us. The tears were there but not flowing. I truly felt empty and helpless. The doctor suggested we get another opinion. We quickly agreed with him. I remember thinking that I should be strong for my wife, but I wasn't sure I knew how. I was learning how very weak I am and that I do not have control of the circumstances of life.

Shortly after that we went to the KU Medical Center in Kansas City. There we met with several different doctors, some of whom were learning how to diagnose the different special needs that children have. They confirmed to us that Tyler indeed had cerebral palsy. They said he would require therapy and special care at home and at school.

The next few weeks were filled with thoughts of what did we do, what could have we done, and why did this *"happen?"* to us. Even some in our church were asking the same questions—some in our presence, some not. Family members struggled with this discovery. It was incredibly difficult to explain. I am sure many people felt sorry for us. Depression took hold of us and rocked us this way and that. *Can the wind howl any louder?* I wondered. *Would the sea refrain from devouring my family?* I'm sure I asked Jesus why He was sleeping when we were about to plunge to the bottom of the sea.

My memory of everything that *"happened"* during those difficult days is foggy at best, but I can tell you that we received more and more grace and peace the more difficult the skies became. I simply was not able to see all the things that God had in store for us. God was still there when we had lost hope. We knew we loved the Lord and also our Tyler with all our hearts. But we could not understand or believe what was *"happening"* to us.

At that point we could not see the other side. The doctors performed various surgeries to help Tyler's eyes and his legs. We discovered the depths of the difficulties new parents with a special-needs child go through during such times. Each time we took him back to the hospital and I had to let go of his little hand, my heart felt like it was truly breaking. We tried to do the things the doctors told us would help him.

My faith at that time was so weak that I waited at least two years before I asked the deacons at our church to pray over Tyler. That *"happened"* because a doctor told us that to help Tyler walk would require inserting bolts into his legs. Those words literally brought me to my knees. We spent time in prayer with those godly men and watched as they laid hands on Tyler. Later another surgeon's diagnosis was that only minor clips of the muscles in strategic locations was necessary. We praised and thanked our Lord for that early miracle. We were humbled by His awesome power to calm us.

Nevertheless, I was the least calm. Robin seemed to deal with these matters so much better than I did.

At this point I want to be as honest as possible: We still cannot see the other side. But our confidence continues to grow. It grows in the Lord, not in us. God uses many things to teach us about what matters most. When I was in high school and before I received eternal life, my friends and I used to drive by a campus built to help kids with hearing problems and needing special therapy. I remember saying, *"That's where crazy people live."* When we moved back to Wichita, KS, to get the help for Tyler that he needed so badly, guess where we lived for six months? The memories of my earlier behavior toward that school haunted me for days.

God is always teaching us and allowing us to go through things to help us trust Him more. Not by accident we found out about Rainbows United, a pre-school for special-needs children in our area. That school was a great source of service for Tyler in his early development. He attended the school for about two years during the mid- to late-1980s. The staff was so helpful in providing intense therapy and wonderful family support. During this time Tyler began to say more words; we knew this was a miracle from God. That is why his terse words today are so special to me. I doubted whether I would ever hear any from him. Robin and I will forever be grateful for this oasis of love and outreach to so many families in crisis.

God also has truly blessed us with a family who has loved Tyler and grown in the Lord right along with every step we have taken. We quickly found out how much of

God's love is in a family that runs to the battle in the Lord's strength—not staying weak or denying that a problem exists, and then breaking apart in defeat.

Through Tyler our Lord has shown His strength to many people. By faith we look toward a distant shore where Tyler will be made whole and our pain will be permanently removed. We know that in heaven together we some day will reach that point.

We asked "what happened?" *not totally sure,*
Our first-born son, disabled with no cure.
The weather got rough, the skies grew dark,
But as time goes on, real fruit leaves its mark.
It is much calmer now; a new front may appear,
But we sail with Jesus and have more strength, not fear.

Chapter 2

UPSET?

Tyler now says many words on a very regular basis. He often asks us to repeat what we have just said to him.

The simple word *"upset"* has a special role in Tyler's life. It has an impact when he says it that needs some additional explanation. It carries with it a special spiritual discernment.

In its regular usage the word *"upset"* seems to reflect only the negative. When Tyler says it, the word seems to have a more positive impact. I want to tell you what I have seen and heard. I do not pretend to think that I have the ability to help anyone stop being *"upset"*, because I do not have that ability. The Bible, however, says a soft answer turns away wrath.

Nevertheless, Tyler can say a word like *"upset"* in such a way that it calms wrath in another person. I try to do this sometimes, but some people are able to stay *"upset"* and always seem to be living with some level of tension in their lives without true peace. I have seen some of them on the road. I have been one of them. I know this much: I cannot do it by saying one word.

Once when Tyler and I were traveling to a baseball game, I was speeding through a "construction zone."

That was not a smart thing to do. Of course, I was not paying attention. When I saw the flashing red lights and heard the siren, I felt upset. I tensed up and said "oh no!" Tyler immediately asked, *"upset?"* I told him that I had just done something wrong. I noticed that his question seemed to have a calming impact on me when he said it.

When the highway patrol officer came to my window, the first person to speak was Tyler. Smiling and leaning over, staring at him, Tyler said, *"My dad's in trouble?"* "Yes, he is", the officer said with a smile—one of "those" all-knowing smiles. Remarkably I got over being *"upset"*, because Tyler spoke the word so peacefully.

The amazing thing is that this kind of reaction happens all the time when Tyler speaks his simple, terse comments.

In the story I just told about the officer, Tyler seemed to help ease an otherwise irritating situation. I've also seen this happen in other situations with Tyler. I know this is a result of God being at work in his life. I believe this is the nature God has given him.

I have not always been as perceptive about how Tyler's words work in the lives of other people. Now when he speaks, I try to listen. I've noticed, for instance, that he seems to speak the right words at the appropriate time. Most people would not give a person with an IQ of 36 that much credit. I give all the glory to God. I know that God can and does use Tyler to bring peace in these situations. That's why I encourage others to look for His peace in any troubling or *"upsetting"* circumstance they may face. God is always ready to help. He is the only source of peace in this world. Tyler has been a key reminder of that to me and other family members.

I went to the dictionary to look up the meaning of the word *"upset"*. I had never really thought about what it meant, though I have experienced its meaning many times. I am amazed at the dictionary's definition: "To overturn, to throw into confusion or disorder, to defeat, unexpectedly. To become overturned."

In Mark 4 we see this word in action. The disciples had been invited by Jesus to "go over to the other side" with Him. As far as they knew, no chance of being unexpectedly overturned or defeated existed. As the sky grew dark and the roughness of the sea began to break over the sides of their boat, the disciples were thrown into disorder and confusion. We can certainly relate to this atmosphere. They got *"upset"* within themselves. Their fear must have grown more intense as they saw their boat filling with water, saw the looks on each other's faces, and heard all the cries of "Woe is me!" Their lack of faith fueled their complaining. The only sign of any calm in the midst of this storm was the fact that Jesus was asleep. When He awoke, He settled them down. By His very presence their expected demise turned into victory. The test they took—in their own strength and without trust in Jesus—was too much for them to pass. They failed to face a difficult circumstance without being *"upset"*.

From "sailing" in our "boat" with Tyler, I draw our personal parallel to this biblical account. Can it be that the one person in our family that the world would call the lesser in quality of life is by far the one who has the greater quality of life—because he is the least *"upset?"*

I see clearly now a picture of our "boat" in the midst

of a great storm—with both Jesus and Tyler asleep in the bow of the ship. I am the one who is *"upset"* as I thrash and worry like the disciples did. All the while Tyler is smiling from ear to ear and swaying (which is something he is famous for doing) side to side with the motion of the boat as it crashes through the winds and the waves. When something occurs that would trouble others, including me, Tyler merely says he will "tell my Supervisor". In Tyler's world, his Supervisor (also known to others as God) is in total control of the boat. No matter how much we may thrash about in the storm, Tyler will move with it. Like the sound of his favorite song, he keeps perfect beat.

I keep asking myself why I am not able to sway that way. At times I cannot even get through a drive-thru at a fast food restaurant without getting *"upset"*. When life's circumstances get tough, I still often say too much, "woe is me" instead of swaying like Tyler does. By this consistent motion Tyler has become quite strong in his upper body. I would be stronger by learning to sway when the way is rough. I wish I could be more trusting and not thrashing.

Most of the time when Tyler asks someone if they are *"upset"*, he is smiling. Our friends and family tell us that his way of asking actually calms them down, too. I believe the word is his way of saying not to let confusion and disorder last too long. Friends and family say Tyler's words help them recognize that their reasons for being *"upset"* are not as important as they might have thought.

I do not recall a time when Tyler asked whether I was *"upset"* when I was not. Somehow he seems to always know. His spirit is so compassionate and pure that God can allow him to see this clearly in others.

Tyler's words and attitude have a very peaceful effect on our family. I believe we experience less long-term stress as a result. I came home one day and sat down in a chair in the living room. Tyler approached me and began to rub my neck. Somehow he seemed to sense that I had experienced a pretty tough day. I am convinced this was God at work! I asked him what he was doing and he said, *"rubbing daddy's neck"*. I felt more relaxed and thanked him for his actions.

I am constantly reminded that what Satan has used to try to overturn us in defeat, God has used to bring glory to Him! How long will it take for me to trust Him completely? I will always be pressing on. Tyler is far ahead in the race of faithfulness.

I hope you can relate to what I am sharing. Too often the world seems to believe a special-needs or handicapped person really does not have a useful place in society. Nothing is more confused and out of touch than that attitude. If we are honest and measure with God's yardstick, we would quickly see that those who truly touch the world with His love and grace include people with special needs. I know for a fact that they are often all ahead of me in this race for the prize! They are the strong and faithful ones! They are the loving and kind ones.

Please do not resist the opportunity to gain peace, love, joy, longsuffering, gentleness, goodness, faith, meekness, and temperance that can arise through one of these precious special-needs or handicapped children. They are examples of what these spiritual fruits look like.

"Blessed are the peacemakers." One of them might ask whether we are *"upset"* and then stay awhile until we are not anymore.

I know beyond a shadow of a doubt that God is using a young man with cerebral palsy to bring peace in our boat that Satan meant to be shipwrecked with no survivors. How awesome is the power of Christ! How proud we are of His servant Tyler! The thunder rolls, the winds howl, and the seas begin to swell. The one- or two-word sentences we hear from Tyler reminds us that all is well.

What the world may call a curse in your life may in fact be God working to produce in you His good fruit. If you have received the free gift of eternal life by faith in Christ and what He did on the cross, He promises that you will be in His boat and nothing you face that *"upsets"* your life will be greater than His ability in you to help you overcome it, and give you rest.

Our daily tests, hard to pass,
And earthly efforts, burn like grass.
When "upset" really describes our way,
It's in Jesus alone we must trust and obey.

The rage of the road is not just a fad,
And it's not just a thing that I think I just had.
It started with the nature in man that's bad,
But can end with Jesus—no more "upset", just glad.

Chapter 3

IT'S NOT TOO BAD?

Tyler began asking the question *"It's not too bad?"* a long time ago. I cannot remember the first time he made the statement. It probably was during a thunderstorm or a tornado warning. We seem to have a number of those in Kansas every year.

I am astounded at the timing of Tyler's short but encouraging words that he says or the questions such as this one that he asks. God has given Tyler a gift to provide encouragement and peace in what he says.

Have different circumstances in our lives caused so much pressure and stress that we have no answer for his question? I know that I get so busy thinking about things and become so occupied with different concerns that I can sometimes even lose track of what I am talking about.

When Tyler is present during a difficult day or an argument or whether someone is hurt or upset, he will ask, "It's not too bad?" I really think he asks it as a question so we can look at the situation and ask ourselves if it is that bad. With Tyler, nothing is too bad. Good weather is something he sees all the time—either the sun is out or it is getting ready to shine. In his world it is either Christmastime or almost Christmastime. The darkness or the storm is never permanent to him. He will not allow anything we face as individuals or as a family to consume us. In the midst of the trial or circumstance, he just quietly asks us or tells us, *"It's not too bad?"*

If your day seems to be reaching an overwhelming stage and waves are closing in on your ship to the point of being a shipwreck, be encouraged that the sun is trying to come out. With Jesus in our ship, nothing is too bad.

Tyler will sometimes say, *"It's not that bad"*, or *"It's a beautiful day"*. Those words will change the course of our ship in a moment. One time in the Christian Life Center at Immanuel Baptist Church Tyler saw one of our friends who had a downtrodden look on her face. Tyler went up to her and asked, *"It's not too bad?"* She turned to him, smiled and replied, "Not anymore Tyler." I don't understand his ability to know people so well, except that this ability is from God.

Tyler constantly tells us that we can face any challenge, because nothing is too bad that we cannot overcome it in Jesus. We need a daily reminder that what we will face today on the lake is "not too bad and certainly not so bad to sink us." Tyler is always there with his beautiful smile. I believe he "prays without ceasing", as Paul wrote, and is in constant communication with Jesus. How else can I explain the timing?

We all need Tyler's attitude in our boats to help us keep from complaining when we think that Jesus is sleeping and does not care that we are perishing. As we travel further out across the lake, more of what we face has become *"not that bad"*, so that we have less fear of the waves and more trust that Jesus can calm the sea.

Robin and I have learned to realize that because of

Tyler's inability to understand how to take care of himself and know enough to be on his own, he will be living with us for the rest of his life—or our lives. When I first began to think about this, the dad in me was disappointed that I would not be going through the "empty nest" with Tyler. But do you know what? *"It's not that bad."*

I know families with many difficult decisions to make. We pray they will find the help they need and get the services necessary to help their children with special needs be as successful in life as possible and reach their full potential. That is what parents with "normal" children want as well. I completely understand this.

Robin and I are not only Tyler's parents, but we also are his legal guardians and trustees. One day the lawyer assigned to Tyler's case visited our house to interview him. We had no idea what Tyler might tell him. Perhaps he did not want us to take care of him or make all of his important decisions for him, so we prayed that all would go according to God's will.

The lawyer was very polite, handed Tyler one of his cards, and told him that if he ever needed him or had any questions, to pick up the phone and call him. Apparently he didn't know Tyler does not use the phone. When the lawyer asked Tyler if he wanted his parents to make all of his decisions for him, Tyler replied, *"Where's my cat?"*

When the lawyer followed up by asking if Tyler wanted to continue living with his parents and allowing us to be in control of his life, Tyler said, *"Where's Molly?"* Molly is the name of our cat.

The lawyer looked at us, smiled, and said that he was finished with his interview. He had heard enough. It was all I could do to keep our other two children, Timothy and Emily, from doing what I was feeling like doing—cracking up. God indeed does have an active sense of humor.

I share this event because while we really don't know what Tyler will say next, we do know whatever he says will be in complete innocence. God allows special-needs children to be born so that He can be glorified—not as punishment to their parents. We need to trust Him completely and to show us in each of these precious lives just how He will work that out. God will always work it out for our good if we love Him. Every good and perfect gift comes down from the Father. Tyler is just one of the many of these good and perfect gifts.

One of our very dear friends, who has loved Tyler from the first time they met, told me one day that we may very well have an angel living with us. It just dawned on me that if that is the case—and I believe it is—it will *"not be too bad"* for us to have an angel live with us for the rest of his life. We certainly appreciate the encouragement we have received over the years from all our family members and friends, many who have shared how much they have grown in the Lord because of knowing Tyler. As Tyler always says to anyone who sneezes, *"bless you!"*

Though the day you just had
Did not make you glad,
Remember what Tyler
Always says to his dad
With Jesus in charge,
"It's not too bad."

Chapter 4

AFTER THIS?

When I was young and our family went on a vacation or to visit extended family or friends, I would ask my dad how long it would be before we would get to where we were going. I am sure he got a little tired of answering that question every 20 minutes or so. After a while, I would finally give up asking my question and just sit back and wait.

As soon as I could sense it was time to leave, which never matched the time my parents were thinking about leaving, I would ask when we were going to leave. I believe this is normal behavior in kids. I also know some kids can be very persistent. Tyler is one of those kids, yet he does this in a much more positive way.

Tyler's level of interest in what happens *"after this"* is second to none. I do not see him ever growing out of this stage of his life. This is critical to his life! His vision of the next event requires us to be ready at a moment's notice with an answer. We have a wall calendar that I try to check on a daily basis. When I forget to do that, I usually just call home and ask Robin what I am supposed to do that evening or where I am supposed to be and at what time. Because of this I am not surprised that Tyler always wants to know what is going on *"after this"*. We recently traveled to the Winter Special Olympic games in Weston, MO, where Tyler gets to compete every year with his friend Bill Cummings, a volunteer with the Kansas Ski Club. They ski together using a sled built especially for special-needs racers. By racer, I mean much less than the 80 mph that the downhill event usually records. Two miles per hour is more like it. Nevertheless this event is certainly another of the many fantastic adventures Tyler gets to experience in his life. We are so thankful for Bill and all of the other wonderful people who give of their time and talents to encourage and assist kids with special needs and help them improve in different areas of sports.

Because of this program we get a firsthand look at what exhilaration means and how much satisfaction occurs in accomplishing any goal. Tyler is always looking forward to what comes next in his life. Still, he doesn't let that stand in his way of finding joy in the present. He loves to go everywhere—whether to a ballgame or swim meet or just a trip to the gas station to get our car serviced. He likes to say they are *"getting the car better?"* He is excited just to be a part of all these different activities or be able to go on an errand that we need to run.

Our family enjoys going on short trips anywhere, any time—for business or for pleasure. These trips give us time to talk. Tyler usually talks to me and I listen intently. Then he talks some more and I listen some more. Tyler will always have something *"after this"*.

As the day ends he is quick to ask us a question he would rather not ask. *"Can't go to bed yet?"* Tyler loves to get the most he can out of each day, so he is never ready for it to end and have to go to bed. When he realizes the time has arrived, he always wants to know what will happen *"after bed?"* When he says this, I am reminded of this verse in Philippians 3:13,14, *"but this one thing I do, forgetting those things which are behind, and reaching forth unto those things which are before, I press toward the mark for the prize of the high calling of God in Christ Jesus."* Tyler always points us to this high calling. He takes no thought of the past (his cerebral palsy). He does not complain about his infirmities or that his legs might be sore or how difficult he finds getting up to stand to be. His compassion is for others who have troubles of their own.

Being mindful of what will come *"after this"* is Tyler's way of asking what his next opportunity will be to see more people and show them how much God loves them. As we go over to the other side with Jesus, one constant remains in our boat: No matter what our circumstances or what we face, we complain less and less about them and more and more press on toward the mark of the high prize. Each difficult circumstance can mean more growth in us and more glory to God!

Tyler has many Special Olympics gold, silver, and bronze medals hanging next to his bedroom door, but his real prize is the high calling in Christ Jesus.

What am I pressing toward? What is my goal? I continue to be amazed that Tyler already has in his grasp this high prize on which I am supposed to be focused. How proud I am! My goal is to trust God to do His work in my life so He can make me the father my kids will be proud of.

What counts most is the status of our relationship with Jesus Christ. Have you trusted Him as your Savior and Lord? Are you in His boat heading to the other side with Him? If so, then *"after this"* is more of the One Tyler is pointing us to: Jesus!

Chapter 5

LIVE ROOM

In a house in which we once lived were some items in the living room that I need to describe before I tell you more about them. I also need to tell you why I believe they have a particular importance to Tyler. Because of these things now I better understand how God can use the simple things in life to teach us so much. Also because of them I easily could have missed the blessings of a simple life lesson.

Tyler called this the *"live room"*. That is the name he still uses. As I began to do some straightening in that room one day, I started to move some things that were on the chair and couch. At first I thought they were just clutter. Instead, I had the urge to sit down and write about them. I knew that the Lord was helping me, so I did not think this was just an excuse to stop cleaning. I knew I could finish cleaning up later.

In front of the window was the Christmas tree. On it at the top was the angel that Tyler helped me attach. While we attached that angel, I saw Tyler stand as straight as I had seen him stand in a while. At the bottom of the tree, only a little water remained in the tree stand. That told me Tyler's girl *"Molly"*, our cat, had been drinking there again.

Sitting on the couch in the *"live room"* was impossible because of all Tyler's stuff on it. I knew I was wrong to even think of cleaning it. Every piece of Tyler's stuff was perched perfectly in its spot and nothing was out of place. The yellow rubber ball with the "smile face" on it reminded me of Tyler's glad heart and sweet spirit. What an example to us of how ours should be as we celebrate the birth of the Lord Jesus, Who not only was born but Who lived for us, then died for us, and now lives again for us!

Next in the pile was a doll dressed in a Christmas outfit. Very cute and colorful she epitomized the kind of girls Tyler hangs around with—mostly his mom, Robin, and his sister, Emily. However, Tyler is not shy at all. He shares his day with anyone and everyone he sees. *"What a positive influence on us all"*, I thought.

"Tango", Tyler's stuffed orangutan, sat by himself in the chair by the tree. Near him was our pillow that says "love makes the warmest nest". The orangutan's name made me think about Tyler dancing. I've never seen Tyler tango, but I am confident he would love to dance if someone asked him. He was not ever supposed to walk but now I have a hard time keeping up with him if he has his eyes on a destination. Once at the finish line during a Special Olympics race his grandpa "Papa" held Tyler's Bible. That was all it took for Tyler to "run" the 25-meter walk to get that Bible and be with Papa. What a symbol! I am sure I do not run to God and His Word like my son ran to his grandpa that day. When that happens, I always marvel that the world calls people like Tyler a 36 IQ. I call it *"for me to live is Christ, to die is more of Christ."*

Tyler lives to be pleasing to Christ! What a pace! I truly think he is winning the race.

At the coffee table Tyler, the best human metronome you can imagine, practices daily, He keeps almost perfect beat to all of his available CD's. The *"live room"* sounds are many, but none more special to Tyler than the CD of the Wyatt Park Christian Church's "A Celebration of Praise." Tyler is proud that his Papa used to play the rhythm guitar in the praise band at the church. Nevertheless, his Papa must work diligently to keep up with Tyler on understanding different beats.

Another member of the praise band is Jason Riley, Tyler's favorite guitar player. Leaning on a pillow next to the piano Tyler has a signed picture of Jason . The CD's that gets the most play is "Come Let Us Worship". That is truly a reminder that Jesus is King of Kings and Lord of Lords. Tyler's love for that CD is a constant reminder for us to worship our Lord all the time.

Two pictures leaning against another pillow on the sofa were taken at Thanksgiving when we went to visit family at my aunt and uncle's house in St Joseph, MO. Smiles were all around! Some very special people to Tyler and our family are in this photo.

That holiday we spent time in my aunt and uncle's *"live room"*. That picture reminded me why every day Tyler keeps lining up different pictures on the couch. He loves people. He loves everyone he meets. One day his display might include a picture of President George W. Bush and beside that a picture of his great grandparents, and next to that a picture of Emily and her 3rd-grade class. Every picture has people in it. His love for people is the reason Tyler says *"hello"* to so many wherever we go. I certainly could learn from Tyler's attitude on that.

The next item on the couch is the Northwest High School Winter Sports program; it is arranged in clear view. Tyler rarely missed a game in which his brother, Timothy, and sister, Emily, played. He was always their biggest fan in the stands. The Northwest staff was always friendly to Tyler and called him by name. Tyler has never met a person who was not his friend. I am amazed at the number of people who come up to shake his hand when we go places. I am no longer Brad but instead "Tyler's dad". I am not even close in this race.

Tyler's sports radio is next on the couch. At a moment's notice it is ready to be switched on to his latest Country favorite. Frankly, I'm not sure where he gets that interest. Many times during the day, Tyler may have as many as three different music sources surrounding us with their tunes. That is just the way it is, and it's OK — well, most of the time.

Lying there next is the current Reader's Digest. His Grandmother Virginia gives him the subscription every year. Tyler keeps the current issue of this magazine as well as the phone book close by. The phone book contains the names of many people, most of whom he has yet to meet.

Yes, our *"Live Room"* is an amazing sight! In every one of our homes Tyler has kept his items in the "Live Room". We have no shortage of things to make a lasting impression on our lives.

I detailed these items in our *"Live Room"* because too much of the time we all are so busy thinking about how difficult our circumstances are and worrying about this thing or that thing that we lose sight of what blessings we have right before our very eyes. We need to open our spiritual eyes and see the calm water that Jesus just made after a storm and through which we can sail right on by to the other side. I'm so glad this room is inside our boat and that we have Jesus with us in it.

The last item in the room that I want to tell you about is the most talked-about piece in Tyler's room. All other things may change in the chair or on the couch, but this one remains the same. On the wall by the front door Tyler keeps a picture of Jesus hanging . Tyler always wants to draw our attention to it. He says *"look"* and points to the picture. Family members will answer, "Who is that?" Tyler responds "my best friend." Tyler always wants to tell us that his best friend likes this or that and that He is happy or upset or sad depending on the situation. I have no doubt that this picture is in our *"live room"* to help Tyler relate to us how much he loves Jesus. He can see his Jesus everyday—and everyday Jesus can see His Tyler. What a wonderful, peaceful, and fulfilling place to be. I am growing in my realization that the cares of this life are but waves that try to rock our boat as we go across to the other side. If we will but look to Jesus, we will find that He is always seeing us, waiting for us to give ourselves to Him, and ready to calm the sea and guide our boat. He gave Himself for us. He will not let us drown. Thanks for joining me here. May His presence be real where you *"live."*

No matter what circumstances you may face,
He is Always there extending grace.
Make very sure your boat's in place
And that He is guiding in every case.

Here is my explanation of what it means to have one's "boat in place"—

The Bible says in John 1:12, *"But as many as received Him, to them gave He the power to become the children of God, even to those who believe in His name."* John 6:47 says, *"Verily verily I say unto you. Believe on the Lord Jesus Christ, and you will be saved."*

Chapter 6

WANT TO WORK THERE

Have you ever visited or driven by a place that you thought would be a great place to work? Over the past few years, our family has experienced many spontaneous verbal work applications to various places where Tyler has a desire to go to *"work there"*.

This particular interest of Tyler's had its beginning at Levy Special Education Center in Wichita, KS. As a student there during his final years of public school he was able to get some valuable training in the school's transition program. What a blessing this was to us! So many people really are "ministering" to special-needs children. We think of them often. Tyler sincerely believes he can *"help people"* in so many ways at these places.

His list of these places is so long it encourages us to be more helpful whenever we have the opportunity. At the university he will *"help the people study books"*. He wants to *"work"* at Missouri Western in St. Joseph, Missouri where PaPa and DeDe (Grandparents) live. At the store, he will *"help people with cash registers"*. If Tyler could *"work"* at the hospital he would *"help the people's legs"*.

At Tyler Road Baptist Church, Tyler said, he will

"help the people sing songs". He does a fantastic job *"working"* as the church *"metronome"*. That is an instrument for indicating tempo in music. How very true that is, because Tyler has the best rhythm around. God really blessed him in this area. Tyler loves to worship the Lord with his rhythm! One time Tyler told me he wanted to *"work"* at Friends University as we were driving by because he wanted to *"help with Special Olympics"*. He had just finished participating in the games, which were held at Friends that year. He remembered how much fun he had with his friends. He thinks he could do that all the time. The importance of Tyler's desire to *"work"* everywhere is not that he just notices where he is and wants to go there. The significance is that he usually says the word *"help"* when he tells us what he wants to do.

I am amazed at his wisdom and the ability he has to constantly remind us of our *"job"*. If he sees a need, he wants to help meet that need.

When we lived in Columbia, MO, in my office we had a rotation schedule at *"work"* to clean the bathrooms in our office. Discussion about that occurred at our home that night. I told the kids I cleaned the bathroom on a particular day. Now Tyler thinks that is what I do every day when I go to *"work"*. He usually says, *"You take the plunger?"* If I have a day off, he says, *"You off tomorrow?"* When I answer *"yes"* he always says *"bathrooms are clean?"* Our family gets a kick out of that; I get to learn lessons in humility.

Tyler is a great teacher. *"Proud of me?"* You bet I am. He is honest and completely sincere. When he first began telling us of his desire to *"work"* almost everywhere he went, we did not realize that he knew what a job would require. As it continued however, we started to understand that his sole reason to do anything at any location was to *"help the peoples"*. I believe that if you look at what we all do in our jobs, it boils down to Tyler's short, three-word sentence, *"help the peoples"*. This young man with an IQ of 36 has amazing abilities to reach out and communicate life's deepest insights.

I have never been a very good listener. Nevertheless, I have learned to make sure I not only listen to Tyler, but I think about what he says. I fear if I don't, I will miss a blessing! I believe we all can do better in this area. Even if someone is not able to speak at all, we can listen with our hearts. Too many missed blessings occur because instead of looking for them, we tend to concentrate on what we think God should have done for us.

God makes ALL things work together for our good, to those who love God, who are called according to His purpose. We continually learn that Tyler is called according to God's purpose. I will tell you that if we don't listen to Tyler, he may call us by other names. Robin could be called *"Uncle Robin"* or I might hear *"Bradley?"* Whatever it takes, Tyler says it.

We were in Columbia, MO, one day when Tyler was preparing to have some dental work done under anesthesia. Before he went to surgery, he saw a lady sitting in the waiting room with a cast on her leg. As we walked by, Tyler asked *"happened?"* to her. She replied that her leg had been broken. Tyler told her *"sorry"*. She smiled at him and thanked him for caring and being sensitive to her. He sets such a pace for us in this race. Most of the time we are not close to competing with him. He does not know any other way to be but genuine and sincere.

Tyler cannot spell his name completely. He can't balance a checkbook. We are still working on him so he can brush his teeth. But he is complete in every way in the area of *"helping peoples"*. Such an attitude is not bound by academic levels or physical attributes. It is a gift from the Lord Who has provided it for us to see firsthand in Tyler.

The Bible says in Galatians 5:22 that . . . *the fruit of the Spirit is love, joy, peace, patience, kindness, goodness, faithfulness, gentleness, self-control. Against such things there is no law.* Evidence of this fruit is living in our home. Even though the world does not give him much rank in life, our God has touched Tyler with an extra measure of His power in the Holy Spirit. We ourselves are not likely to attain his level of pure walking with Jesus.

When we need help, Tyler points to his *"Supervisor"*. I looked up this word in the dictionary. It says, "Someone who directs or oversees." Tyler has not always called Jesus his Supervisor, because he used to call him his *"Best Friend"*. I believe the Lord is using Tyler to teach yet another lesson—because as we make our Lord the One who directs us, we learn more and more not to trust ourselves.

I am reminded of Proverbs 3:5, 6. We know Jesus is our best friend, but He wants to direct us and oversee all we do. We must completely trust Him to do that through all of our circumstances, regardless of life's "weather".

During the storms of life, Jesus wants to be your

"Supervisor", too. When the seas are calm, look to Him to direct and oversee your life. Tyler has that trust. As we trust Him more, He will *"work"* out His will for us and give us His power to *"help peoples"*. We are proud that Tyler wants to *"work"* everywhere. We pray that God will open doors and make a way for many to have this same job, with the same *"Supervisor"*.

There is so much work yet to be done,
And many souls, yet to be won.
As we labor in our field,
It's to our "Supervisor" *we yield.*
It's my job to keep on planting,
And the Lord's, eternal life granting.

Chapter 7

IT'S NOT ALL MY FAULT?

I have the reputation of being able to precisely locate with my vehicles most of the available deer population in our area. I have successfully demonstrated my ability to hit these deer during late night and also in broad daylight. I am not proud of this fact. The first time I hit a deer, I was in Missouri traveling alone. The accident did not leave much noticeable damage, but we traded the car because it never lost the "deer smell" inside.

The next incident occurred while Tyler, Timothy and I were on our way home from a baseball tournament in Enid, OK. Since the weather was so nice, I am sure it was difficult for the deer to miss us! The airbags deployed. Tyler was in the front seat. He was bruised on his face pretty badly. Some of his bruises may have been the result of all the toys and stuffed animals that he likes to sit in front of him on the dashboard.

We were so thankful that no one was seriously injured in the accident; we all had our seat belts fastened. We will not soon forget the first aid our friend, a nurse, gave to Tyler after it *happened*. She and others were following us home. She was quick to provide an ice pack for his cheek. We were able to caravan home with another family we knew who were close by. We had to make a few stops along the way to fill the damaged radiator with water and antifreeze. We have a different van now, but Tyler still remembers that incident. It comes up every once in a while, especially when we drive by the *"deer"* signs and Tyler tells me it is *"not all my fault"*. In this case he means himself. I really don't know why he says that, but a few things have entered my mind. Since the accident he has repeated this statement numerous times and always during certain challenges we are facing.

You and I know we are not in control of our circumstances. Things take place everyday to which we react. Some of these are very difficult situations. During such times in his life Tyler will say *"it's not all my fault"*. He will say it if his siblings are in trouble or the umbrella in the back yard falls over. He will say it when he uses all the ice for drinks or spills something. Robin always tells him it is not his fault—and of course it isn't. Other things have happened that are not his fault. The fact that Tyler is handicapped is not his fault.

Tyler's statements remind me of the passage in John 9:1-5. Jesus' disciples ask Him about a man they saw who was blind from birth. They asked, *". . . who had sinned, this man or his parents that he was born blind?"* Jesus responded *"neither this man nor his parents sinned, but this happened so that the work of God might be displayed in his life."* This passage means so much to us as we continue to grow in the Lord and as He shows us more of His will for Tyler's life. Tyler is an awesome example of what a stress-free life looks like.

I know there is so much more temptation these days to

place blame, find fault, and build pressure in our lives. God's will is not that we do this. The truth is that we cannot get the true peace and love we need from this world, because our problems are spiritual. While not recognizing this, we too often seek physical, financial, or other solutions. Thank God He solved our problem in His Son Jesus Christ. Even though our sinful nature certainly wasn't His fault, He took our entire fault on Himself to the cross. He provided the only way for us to become free of this fault.

I used to wonder whether Tyler understands how to receive eternal life. At one point I thought he had some responsibility in making that spiritual decision, but I don't any more. Our Lord Jesus Christ, in His divine wisdom, great power, and love, has set me totally free as to Tyler's place in eternity. I know in my heart Jesus has prepared a place for me. I also know beyond doubt He is taking special care in getting Tyler's room ready, too. Maybe that is really why Tyler says this sentence so much! *In Christ, we become clean and without fault, set free from sin!*

> *He might not talk as great as he could*
> *Or walk like you and I think that he should.*
> *But really watch and listen if you would*
> *And see and hear all that Jesus made good.*

Fault is defined as "worthy of blame, misdeed, and imperfection or defect; responsibility for an error or misdeed."

We are worthy of all blame, *"but God demonstrated His love for us, in that while we were yet sinners, Christ died for us."* Romans 5:8.

God gave me this poem after meeting a mother and her special-needs child. She told me that her husband had left them shortly after the news that her child had problems. This is what he missed. When Tyler gets to do something or go somewhere and I am not there, he tells me *ya missed it*.

Ya Missed it

He had his plans, his son was brand new.
Their future awaits, all his dreams would come true.
He had no way of knowing that those difficult days,
Would cause so great a pressure,
It might crush him if he stays.

He has a son who is special, not "normal"
    or like him,
Then everything so bright was suddenly dim.
He left shortly after; his family was split,
And he might not really know this yet,
    but he's missed it!

He has missed his son's hugs, his thank yous,
    and his smile,
And he's missed seeing all the people
Who have been changed by his style.
He will miss being there for his wife,
To help her care for their son's life.

And he'll miss seeing all the faces, of the people
    who get the joy,

And he won't ever know, it was the result of his boy.
I am sure had he stayed and found out what is true,
He would be much stronger now,
More like the son he once knew.

There is still time to see it,
Only there must be certain change,
On the throne of his heart is where Jesus must sit,
Or he'll forever regret to have missed it.

Chapter 8

YOU HAPPY?

One thing I know for sure: We all have the same amount of time during the day. Based on our different circumstances we all constantly make choices about how to spend those days . These choices are a result of such things as our beliefs, convictions, and how we were reared.

Today a greater gulf seems to exist between those who are truly happy and those who are not. Recognizing people who really love life is easy—they are filled with joy in their daily walk. Too few of them exist. In James 1:2 the Bible says to *"consider it all joy when you encounter various trials."* These trials we face today will likely bring out the best or the worst in us. We always have a choice.

And so it is with eternal life. Jesus died for all of us. He gave us all the choice. To receive the free gift that was paid for by Jesus Christ is to know what joy really is in life. No matter what we face, He gives the grace to overcome anything and leaves a smile in our spirit in the end. He puts it there. From the beginning Tyler has been a happy child. Many people have said this about him. It shows in his sweet smile. He shines!

Because of his disability Tyler has a high threshold of pain. We continue to work with him to get him to stop biting his fingernails. Despite our efforts his nails seem to stay on the borderline of infection. When I bring it up, he asks me, *"you happy?"* He means I am probably not.

Tyler is always happy to see someone, no matter who that person is. Everyone is a friend for life with Tyler.

He has the authority to ask anyone *"you happy?"* I need to be honest about this. Yes, at times we do feel his wrath. These are very minor events to us. He does some things that under normal circumstances would be annoying in a family. For instance, he always wants to sit in the front seat of any vehicle in which he is riding. When I was in high school, we used to call this "riding shotgun". We've learned through the years that we don't dare put him in any other seat in the vehicle. Timothy and Emily understand this from first-hand experience. Tyler also must have all of his favorite things with him when he goes to bed. This includes his stuffed bears, phone book, portable radio, wristbands, or whatever he asks for. He has pretty simple demands, but they had best be met.

Spending time with people is important to Tyler—he is all happiness and smiles from ear to ear. He asks of us his question *"you happy?"* at the most interesting times— always when we need to be reminded to be happy. We all need this, since the weather may change above us at any moment and circumstance may upset us and steal the joy in our lives.

Tyler is always there to encourage and to add the precious air to an otherwise deflated balloon. He may ask where your wife is, call your kids by name, or even ask about your pet or the car he knows you drive. You can always count on his smile and his genuine interest in your life. He smiles as he faces the storms. He does not complain as so many of us "normal" people do. The reason he can smile is that he sees the sun beyond the clouds. He knows in his heart the sun will shine soon.

When you can have that kind of vision, you are not usually a candidate for the question, *"you happy?"* People know that you are.

What I have described are things I have seen and heard but cannot fully understand. I do know that we do not ask Tyler *"you happy?"* very much. We already know the answer. We often lack this consistency in our lives. He is wise in God's eyes and understands life as Jesus desires him to—with a 36 IQ. That is all I need to know.

I keep hearing him say, *"Proud of me?"* I am thinking that I need to start asking him if he is *"proud of me?"*, too. I have more to be proud of than he does. The question for all of us is, *"are we happy?"* Tyler wants you to be as he is.

Fulfilling days will return again
When our deepest desire is to have joy within.
Take Jesus in your boat—His forgiveness of sin,
Then Tyler will ask "You happy?", and you grin.

Hi—from TY
Sittin' and swayin',
That's what I do.
Seein' all the people,

Wonderin' about you.
I've seen a lot,
Been around a while,
Please glance at me,
I'll show you my smile.
Hi—from Ty**

**written while sitting in the car waiting with Tyler in a grocery-store parking lot—just watching him as he waits for his mom and observing all the people that enter and leave the store.

Chapter 9

MY BEST FRIEND

Clearly Tyler will ask questions for as long as he is Tyler.

He also wants us to know that no matter what the day brings, his "*best Friend*" Jesus is with us. Jesus is with Tyler when he is walking, in the shower, sleeping, praying, eating, and everywhere else. Tyler constantly asks us what his "*best Friend*" is doing. He wants to know if Jesus is proud of him. He asks it this way; *Jesus proud of me?*

We count it pure joy when we see Tyler's face light up at the mention of his "*best Friend*". The fact that we know Jesus loves Tyler more than we ever could simply rights our ship. You see, Tyler's priorities are in order; he is a special-needs child. This child is 28-years old. What the world might call *insufficient* is with us in all sufficiency, spiritually speaking. The world is focused on the physical aspects of life and what pleases the senses. Our living example sees what lies ahead on the other side. He looks forward to going there. The situation is pretty simple to Tyler. He and his "*best Friend*" are close. They understand each other. He makes me ask myself, *Do my priorities line up more closely with his, and His, or my own and the cares of this life?*

When we talk about someone who is hurting and needs our prayers, Tyler is quick to say, *"Tell my best friend."* And then we do.

Conversations between Tyler and his *"best Friend"* may be short, but nothing keeps his prayers from being heard. Jesus longs for us to pray that way. Too many of us have too many selfish desires in the way.

Another reason our prayers are not answered is that we do not ask at all. It boils down to motives and priorities. In James 1 the Bible says if we really want wisdom, which is having the knowledge of what is right and doing it, we should ask God. Then when we ask, we must really believe He will answer. We must not doubt that He will. If we doubt, we will be like someone in a boat on the sea. We will be tossed about without any direction. Only when we are with Jesus in His boat is true direction in life possible. We must choose to put all of our trust in Him.

The leader in this race is upstairs listening to his favorite CD of the day and glancing over on the wall to make eye contact with the Jesus in the picture hanging by our front door. They both are all smiles. Tyler and Jesus are *"best friends"*. The One, who paid the greatest price of all, reaches down in wisdom to live in a child and extend this *"Best Friend"* grace to us.

He is our Friend and gave Himself for us,
For Tyler in his way, there is no fuss.
Look no farther than the plan so needed
And accept this Friend. For your life He pleaded.
He calls from His boat to please climb in.
And sail with Him—your true "BEST FRIEND".

Chapter 10

PROUD OF ME?

I have titled all of the chapters in this book with short sentences that Tyler says consistently. None has been more important to me than this one.

Robin and I have been blessed to have three beautiful children. Tyler has a younger brother, Timothy, who loves him dearly. He is a wonderful example of what a patient and kind younger brother is like. We three guys enjoy attending baseball games together. One time we got tickets to see the Kansas City Royals play. Our seats were in the "nose-bleed section". We could barely get Tyler to his seat because the steps were so steep. About midway through the game, Timothy turned to me and said, "Dad, when I play here, I am going to make sure Tyler sits down there." He pointed to the spot right behind the Royals dugout. At the time Timothy was about 5 or 6. *"Proud of me?"*

When we are in public, Timothy has always looked out for Tyler. He gave Tyler a hug and a kiss every night. Timothy told his mother one time that if anything happened to Robin and me, he would take care of his older brother. At the time Timothy was about 14. Timothy never complained when he was asked to help with his brother.

Timothy also was very focused and successful in the classroom. He was honored as one of the top students at Northwest High School. He was active in the Fellowship of Christian Athletes. He also was a member of the National Honor Society. I believe God must have extended this mental grace to every other generation. I asked him one time if I could help him with his math (calculus!). He told me I could "turn up the light a little." That was an honest answer, but I was thinking I could do more. Timothy was blessed to be able to play baseball in college. As a sophomore pitcher at Neosho County College he was given the title Academic All America. He finished up at Kansas State University, is married now, and is working as a Certified Public Accountant. His wife, Amber, is Tyler's *girlfriend*—and she is OK with that. We are truly blessed to have her in our family. The most important thing about Timothy is that he is learning to sway Tyler's way in the boat with Jesus. The Lord is growing the fruits of the Spirit into Timothy. For that we always will be thankful. We could not be more proud of him and his love for his Lord and his brother.

Tyler has a little sister named Emily who really was *little* when she arrived in our family. She was born three months before we expected her to be here. Robin developed pregnancy-induced hypertension, so Emily had to be delivered early in order for Robin to live. God extended greater grace and brought peace in the midst of this raging storm by allowing both Robin and Emily to stay with us! The drug Surfactant was just being introduced. Emily was given it to help her lungs develop quickly. At that time only very few hospitals had access to this drug.

What perfect timing our God has! Emily weighed 2 pounds 4 ounces when she was born but dropped to 1 pound 16 ounces a few days later.

We spent the next 70 days after her birth in and out of the hospital visiting Emily and taking care of our two boys. Our family and friends were always there to support us. We will forever be thankful for this.

We especially appreciated some good friends who let us use their video camera so we could record video of Emily's progress. Through it all Emily was a real fighter. Of course God also was in control. *Proud of me?* She just celebrated her 20th birthday. While her lungs were not developed fully at birth, they work very well now!

Emily has a deep desire to make sure Tyler is treated fairly. She is his chief defender. He loves hanging out with his *sweet girl* and her boyfriend Brian. When Emily was very young, Tyler one time arrived home from the hospital after surgery on his legs. He was in a cast. When she saw him, she began to cry. She said she "didn't want him to hurt". *Proud of me?*

Emily loves to hug Tyler. She watches out for him to make sure he is safe. She also attended Northwest High, was a member of the National Honor Society, and on the cross-country and swim teams. She now is a junior at Wichita State University. Her freshman year in college she attended the University of Nebraska at Kearney on a swimming scholarship. I was not kidding about how good her lungs are. She comes in a close second to Tyler in the "outgoing" category. Maybe she is tied with her mom.

When she was about 7, Emily wrote these words about Tyler: "Hi, I'm Emily. Tyler is my older brother. He is handicapped, but it doesn't bother me. My brother is funny, sweet, and kind. But sometimes he can be really mad. But I still love him. He always says when someone is mad, *upset?* Whenever he comes into my room, he turns on my music player and my light. It doesn't bother me that much. But when he turns it to Country, now that bothers me. He says he doesn't want to go to Grandma's house, but when he gets there he is so happy. Whenever he gets a chance to shake someone's hand, he always squeezes it. I love my brothers. Oh yeah, I forgot to tell you I have another brother but he can tell you about himself. My brother Tyler uses a walker sometimes to get around. I love my brother. I also like it when he says he loves me so much, too."

I am especially proud of Emily for her compassion. Being around special-needs children can bother some people. She, on the other hand, is a wonderful example of how we are to love and care for them.

We are grateful for the three children God has given us! We are learning that nothing can sink us. This is the work that God began in us. He has promised to continue to do this good work in us and in all those who sail in their boats with Jesus. He keeps bringing me back to this passage and others which contain the promise of hope for the future in our boat. As we face each new day with its surprises and opportunities, nothing can keep us more at peace than Jesus can. For me to know His boat will never sink and those in it will never drown is enough. No problem we encounter is too great for Him to calm.

As long as I remain here in the flesh, in the same way Tyler does I must be faithful in pointing people to Jesus. I know I must encourage others to get into His boat, receive His eternal life, and then trust in Him no matter how much the weather may try to rock their boats. The other side will be worth it all.

I know Robin, Tyler, Timothy, Emily, and I will see Jesus and spend eternity forever with Him. As we look to His side, we know we will see our Tyler holding the strong hand of Jesus. He will have that sweet smile that has encouraged so many. We will hear him ask, *"My best Friend Jesus proud of me?"* He will wear no braces. He will continue that special smile when he hears his Supervisor say to him, "Well done thou good and faithful servant!" We will hear Tyler thank Jesus for letting him help all who knew him understand the joy and content- ment available no matter what they faced in this life. He will say that if he was able to encourage one person to let Jesus steer his or her boat and be his or her guide to the other side, then his living was worth it all.

Indeed, I've experienced joy writing about how God can take what Satan meant for our destruction and used it for His glory and honor. This is the message I wanted to share with you, my readers. Wherever you are in your life, I know He can bring true peace to you right now. If you are willing to trust Jesus as your Savior and Lord, you are in His boat. He promises you will "go to the other side".

Much of my life I stood on the shore
Not knowing in my heart there was so much more.

He called out my name and took me with Him,
And forever I'll be where it's not sink or swim.

There are many problems you see as too tall.
There are the solutions that still make you fall.
God gave His own Son, not a plan for a season,

The cross was His payment; we are His reason.

Family Photo Album

Robin, Tyler, and Brad pose in the family's home.

Tyler asks, "Proud of Me?"
and his author-father says absolutely he is.

The Russell siblings and their significant others
are pictured from left to right, Brian, Emily, Tyler,
Amber, and Timothy. Tyler is special to each one
of them and they are to him, too.

Sister Emily always has
been proud of and loved
her big brother, Tyler.

Tyler poses with his "Sweet Girl" Emily.

Tyler and his friend, Bill, enjoy the activities at the Winter Special Olympics.

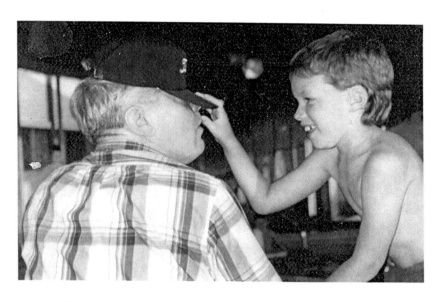

Tyler and his Papa share a moment together.

Tyler wears his favorite t-shirt.

Tyler and his buddies relax after a game.

Tyler and his dad walk to the bus—
something Tyler's doctors said he would
never be capable of doing.

Order more copies of

Proud of Me?

Call toll free: 1-877-212-0933
Visit: www.crosshousepublishing.org
Email: crosshousepublishing@earthlink.net
FAX: 1-888-252-3022
Mail copy of form below to:
CrossHouse Publishing
P.O. Box 461592
Garland, TX 75046

Number of copies desired _____

Multiply number of copies by $ 9.95

Subtotal _____

Please add $3 for postage and handling for first book and add 50-cents for each additional book in the order.

Shipping and handling$_____

Texas residents add 8.25% sales tax $_____

Total order $_____

Mark method of payment:

check enclosed _____

Credit card# _____

exp. date_____ (Visa, MasterCard, Discover, American Express accepted)

Name _____

Address _____

City State, Zip _____

Phone _____ FAX _____

Email _____

LaVergne, TN USA
04 October 2010
199507LV00002B/1/P